COLLECTORS GUIDE

To

COCA-COLA ITEMS

Photography by Don Miller
Marion, Indiana

Published by
L-W Book Sales
P.O. Box 69
Gas City, IN 46933

Table of Contents

Al Wilson

Al Wilson has been a salesman most of his life, and rates a masters in his field. Nineteen years ago, he bought his first Coca-Cola tray for $1 - sold it for $20 - and the buyer turned it for $70. His interest peaked. There were no price guides then. Atlanta was part of his territory, and eventually he found an underground store that sold Coca-Cola items. Here he got his first ideas on cost and price. He frequented the Archives, also. Although they had many stories to tell, there was just a whiff of any keepsakes to exhibit and limited knowledge of their value. Several books have now been written that include most of the rare collectibles we know about today.

SO WHY ANOTHER PRICE GUIDE? Al has bought and sold more original Coca-Cola memorabilia than anyone else, including 90% of the pieces listed in other books. He would rather sell than collect, and has been known to pull a prize from his own collection to sell - just for the thrill of it. This price guide (Vol. 1) will reflect his years of selling in and out of the country to the novice and the entrepreneur.

A Guide To Grading

MINT OR NEW CONDITION — No trace of handling. Absolutely new. To be in this condition, tray or sign would have to be found in original wrapper.

EXCELLENT, NEAR NEW CONDITION — Appears to be new, but on close examination will have hairlines on the surface of the tray or sign. Minor paint chipping on the rim or edges. Many dealers call this mint, it is not. Mint is new.

FINE CONDITION — A fine tray, sign or other item will have minor hairline scratches on surface, medium paint chipping on edge, very minor fading, possibly a faint ring stain or stain, no rust.

VERY GOOD CONDITION — Minor scratches or flaking, ring stains or stains, minor fading of color. Very minor dents, rust, if any, must be minor, pin head size, not on main part of picture.

GOOD CONDITION — Small scratches or pitting, small dents, small rust spots. Not usually collected unless an early or rare tray or sign.

Note

Special attention should be given to this grading guide. Many dealers and collectors have a tendency to over-rate condition of an item. Particular attention should be given to the fading of an item. Throughout the years, many signs and trays have faded. In most cases, sunlight or just plain light have caused the items to fade. Fading in some cases has caused items to turn a completely different color. This is confusing for the person who has never seen the item in new condition.

Serving, Change, & Tip
TRAYS

1901 Change Tray
6" Dia.

1906 Med. Oval
10½" x 13¼"

1909 Med. Oval
10 c/4" x 13"

1910
10½" x 13¼"

1905 Vienna Art Plate
Frame & Box
Wood, Tin, Plaster

1903 Hilda Clark
Tin 15" x 18½"

1913
10½" x 13¼"

1913 Oval
12½" x 15¼"

1914
10½" x 13¼"

1914 Oval
12½" x 15¼"

1917 Oblong
8½" x 19"

1920 Oval
13¾" x 16½"

1920
10½" x 13¼"

1921
10½" x 13¼"

1922
10½" x 13¼"

1923
10½" x 13¼"

1924
10½" x 13¼"

1925
10½" x 13¼"

1926
10½" x 13¼"

1927
10½" x 13¼"

1927
10½" x 13¼"

1929 (Glass)
10½" x 13¼"

1928
10½" x 13¼"

1929 (Bottle)
10½" x 13¼"

1930 (Telephone)
10½" x 13¼"

1930
10½" x 13¼"

1931 (Rockwell)
10½" x 13¼"

1932
10½" x 13¼"

1933 Francis Dee
10½" x 13¼"

1934
10½" x 13¼"

1935
10½" x 13¼"

1936
10½" x 13¼"

1937
10½" x 13¼"

1938
10½" x 13¼"

1939
10½" x 13¼"

1940
10½" x 13¼"

1941
10½" x 13¼"

1942
10½" x 13¼"

1948
10½" x 13¼"

1950's
10½" x 13¼"

1909 Tip
4¼" x 6"

1905 Tip
4" Dia.

1907 Tip
4¼" x 6"

1910 Tip
4¼" x 6"

1913 Tip
4¼" x 6"

1914 Tip
4¼" x 6"

1917 Tip
4¼" x 6"

1920 Tip
4¼" x 6"

1914 Self Framed Betty Tin
31" x 41"

1907 Relieve's Fatigue Trolley Sign
11" x 20½"

1930's Sign Procelain
12" x 31"

1932 Sign 5 Color Porcelain
10" x 30"

1926 Sign RARE Coca-Cola Outlined in Green Porcelain
10" x 30"

1920's Sign Mfg. Dasco Tin
5¾" x 17¾"

1932 Reverse Painting Sign Glass
11" Dia.

1933 Sign Tin
19½" Dia.

1933 Bottle Sign 5 color Tin
11½" x 34½"

1926 Bottle Sign 5 color Tin
12" x 35"

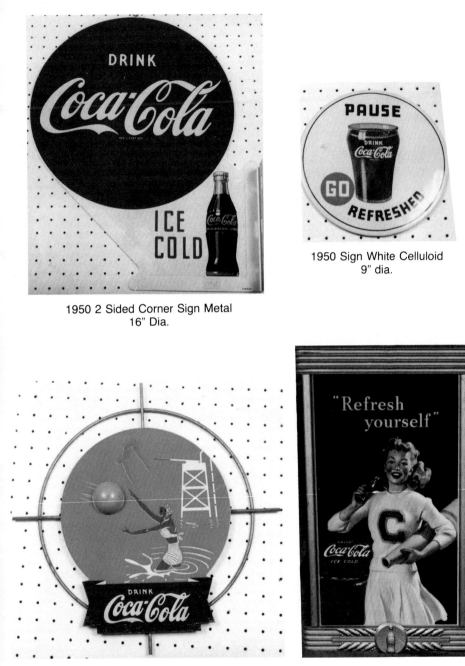

1950 2 Sided Corner Sign Metal
16" Dia.

1950 Sign White Celluloid
9" dia.

1930 Sign Masonite in Metal Frame
16"

1944 Cheerleader Sign
Cardboard Frame
15" x 27"

1935 2 sided Triangle Sign
Porcelain

1930 Triangle Sign w/ applied bottle
Plywood

1940's Sign-Triangle w/ arrow Plywood

1930's Sign White Porcelain
18"

1950's Cash Register Sign Glass w/wood base
11"

1960's Sign Tin
20" x 28"

1939 2 Sided Sign
Porcelain
25¼" x 26¼"

1950's Sign Celluloid
9" Dia.

Will Return Sign Brass
6" x 6"

1950's 6 Pack Sign Tin
11" x 12"

1950's 6 Pack Sign Tin
11" x 12"

1932 Sign Tin
3 Feet

1930's Bottle Sign Porcelain
12½"

1950's Convex Sign Metal
6 Feet

Sprite Boy Booth Light Plastic
4½" x 6"

1931 Bottle x-mas Sign
Tin Embossed
4½" x 12½"

Disc with 50th Anniv. Celluloid
9"

Disc "Delicious & Refreshing 1950's Celluloid
9"

Sprite Box Arrow Sign (3 Pieces)
Masonite and Wood
30"

1930's 2 Piece Sign Plywood & Masonite   8" x 26" each piece

1950's Sign Plywood & Masonite   12" x 16"

1927 2 sided Arrow Sign Tin

1932 Sign 5 Color Tin
19½" Dia.

1930's Sign Cardboard
12" x 16"

1926 Sign Tin
8½" x 11"

1927 Sign Tin
8½" x 11"

1927 Sign Tin
8½" x 11"

1950's Clock & Lighted Sign
9" x 20"

1950's Motion Lighted Sign Water Falls
9" x 20"

1950's Motion Lighted Sign PAUSE
9" x 20"

1950's Stand Up Lighted Sign 2 sided

1950's 1 Gal. Syrup Can
Metal-paper label

1949-1953 Radio (Cooler Shape) Bakelite

Chalk board Menu Tin
19" x 27"

1930 Menu Board Wood
13½" x 24¾"

Menu Mirror Glass
2¼" x 3⅜"

50th Anniv. Menu Mirror Glass
2¼" x 3⅜"

1931 Calendar Celluloid
2" x 3"

Wall Sconce Cardboard
9" x 12"

6 Rack Bottle Holder Metal
43" High

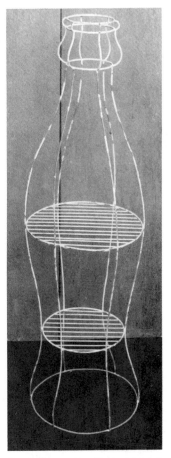

Bottle Frame (for display) Metal
16" Dia. x 42" High

1970's Dispenser
White Ceramic

Match Strike Porcelain
4½" x 4½"

Padlock Key Brass
1½" x 1½"

1930's String Holder Tin
16" High

Push Plate Embossed
1930's Porcelain
2¼" x 35"

Push Plate 1950's
Porcelain 3" x 32"

1940's Push Plate
Raised Letters Porcelain
3" x 31½"

Push Plate 1950's
Porcelain 4" x 29¾"

Push Plate (Silhouette
Girl) Metal
3½" x 33"

Push Plate 1940's
Raised Letters Porcelain
3" x 31½"

Push Plate 1930's
Porcelain 4" x 28"

Push Plate Raised
Letters Metal 1950's
3" x 40"

Push Plate 1950's Metal
3" x 6"

Door Pull Metal Frame
Plastic Bottle

Door Pull 1950's Aluminum

Push Plate Porcelain
4" x 8"

Push Plate 1960's
Metal 4" x 8"

Push Plate 1930's
Porcelain 3½" x 13½"

Push Plate Porcelain
4" x 11½"

Push Plate Porcelain
4" x 11½"

Calendar for each Year Listed in Price Guide

1973 Big Wheel
Red & White Box Metal

1960's Box Car (will go with Coca-Cola Train)
Red & White Plastic

1970 Truck
Red & Beige Plastic

Metal Craft Truck Rubber
Wheels / Working Headlights

Truck with Fold Down
Sides Plastic

Marx Truck with Horn on Cab 1950's Metal
12" Long

Truck (Hong Kong)
1960's Plastic
4½" Long

Truck Zip-A-Long
with Man 1970
Plastic 4½" Long

Truck Wind-Up
(Hong Kong)
1970's Plastic
3½" Long

V-W Van with Man in Cab Friction
Tin 8½" Long

Truck (Japan)
Friction 1970's
Plastic 4¾" Long

1 Budgie Truck Metal 5¼"

2 Friction Truck (Japan) Tin 1950's
   5" Long

3 Pyro Truck Plastic 1940's 5½" Long

4 Match Box Truck Metal Black Wheels
   1950's 2½"

5 Match Box Truck Metal 2½"
   Staggered Cases Grey Wheels

6 Match Box Truck Grey Wheels
   Metal 2½" Long

7 Truck Plastic 1⅞" Long

8 Friction Truck (Japan) 1950's Tin
   4" Long

9 Friction Truck (Japan) 1950's Tin
   4¼" Long

10 Friction V-W (Van) 1950's Tin
    4" Long

11 Linemar Friction Truck 1950's Tin
    2¾" Long

12 Friction Truck Multi-Color Tin
    1¾" Long

13 Friction Truck (Japan) 1950's Tin
    4" Long

Van (V-W) 1950's Tin 8½"   Friction Truck Bottles   Friction Truck 1950 Tin
                              pull out from sides   8"
                              1950's Tin 8" Long

Truck Berliet Stradair   Truck Bedford by Dinky   Truck 1970's Plastic
Frame Metal 4" Long   1950's Metal   3⅜" Long

Metal Craft Truck Rubber   Metal Craft Truck
Wheels Metal   Metal Wheels Metal

1950's Marx Truck Yellow Metal

1940's Smith Miller Truck   Marx Truck Wood Blocks Red Metal
Wood Blocks Red Metal

Zip Along Truck White Plastic

1950's Sprite Boy Truck Boxed Yellow Metal

1960's Buddy L Truck - Boxed Yellow Metal

1960's Friction Car w/box
Red & White Metal

1950's Battery Operated Truck w/box
Yellow & White Metal

1950's Yellow Truck Plastic

1950's Yellow Truck Plastic (open sides)

1940's Sprite Boy Truck Metal

Baseball Bat Wood 32" Long

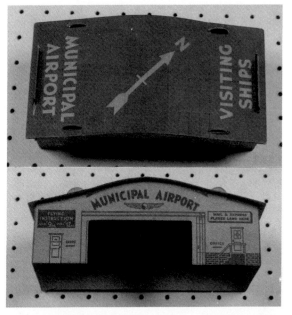

Airport Toy Bldg. 2 pieces Cardboard Yellow & Red

1930's Bang Gun Cardboard   101 Magic Tricks   1932 10th Olympiad 2 sides
Cardboard 5½" dia.

1930 Yo Yo Edwards Mfg. Co.
Cincinnati OH Wood 1¾"

1950's Vending Bank w/box   1950's Dispenser Battery Operated
Plastic - Transparent 5½"   Working Cond. Tin 6½" x 9½"

1930's Beanie Felt 8" dia.   1950's Bank Tin 2¼" x 3¾"

Etched Mirror w/Bottle 1920's Glass   Ingot (Cincinnati OH) 75th Anniv.
8" x 11½"   Silver

1950's Transistor Radio Vending
Machine Plastic 2⅜" x 4½"   Original Stuffed Santa 1940's Cloth

Buddy Lee Doll (orig. uniform)
Plastic 12" High

1920's Signed Property of Coca-Cola Co.
Leaded Glass Tiffany Type 18" Dia.

Milk Glass Shade or Globe 16" dia.

1920's Bottle Lamp Coca-Cola
Embossed on base glass 20" high

Milk Glass Shade Procelain
Fixture 8"

1920's Gilbert Regulator Wood

1930's Clock Brass Mantle
w/glass Dome 6" x 9"

Round Chime Clock
Oak Wood 15½" dia.

German Travel Clock Brass
3" x 3"

Pocket Mirrors

1910

1909

1908

1906

1905

1922

1920

1916

1913

1911

1930's Pretzel Dish Aluminum

1930 Sandwich Plate Knowles China Co. 7¼"

Taylor & Smith & Taylor China Dinnerware
White w/ red trim

1940 Ash Tray
w/Gold Cig. Lighter Attached
Metal 5"

1950's Ashtray tin
5¼" dia.

50th Anniv. Ashtray
Metal 3⅜" Squ.

Ash Tray w/ decals &
Orig. Matches Bakelite
Tray Metal Bottle

1950's Ash Tray (High &
Low) Tin 5¼" dia.

Embossed Banded Dish
1940's w/ hand holding bottle
Metal 4" dia.

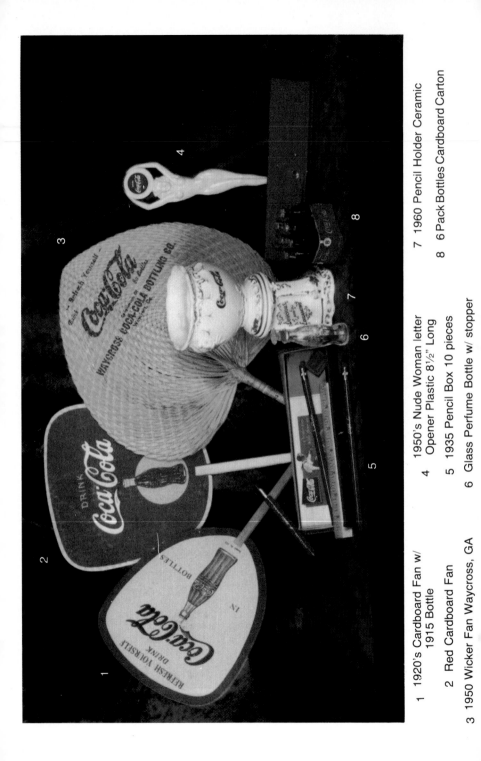

1 1920's Cardboard Fan w/
   1915 Bottle

2 Red Cardboard Fan

3 1950 Wicker Fan Waycross, GA

4 1950's Nude Woman letter
   Opener Plastic 8½" Long

5 1935 Pencil Box 10 pieces

6 Glass Perfume Bottle w/ stopper

7 1960 Pencil Holder Ceramic

8 6 Pack Bottles Cardboard Carton

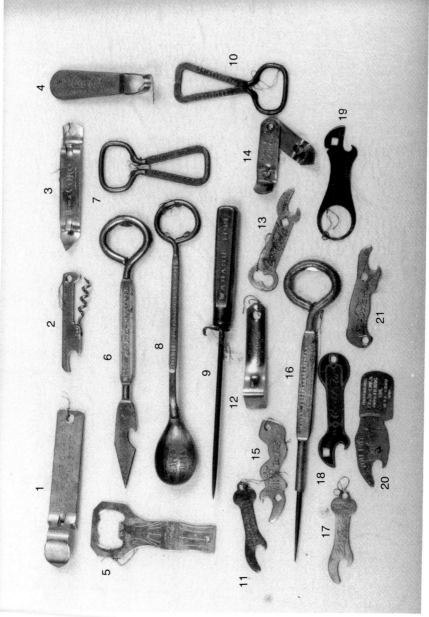

1 1960's Scripto Lighter
2 1960's Lighter
3 1950's Zippo Lighter in Box
4 1950's Rosen Lighter

5 1960's Lighter Chatanooga Btgl. Co.
6 1950's Bottle Lighter Pull Apart
7 1950 Lighter Dispoz.-A-Lite
8 1950's Balboa Lighter

9 1950's Lighter
10 1960's Lighter Parr
11 1960's Lighter Zippo Applied Bottle
12 1960's Lighter Scripto

13 1950's Lighter Rosen
14 1960's Lighter Supreme

1905 Trade Card or METAMORPHIC

Blotters listed in Price guide,
left to right top to bottom

1917 Senate or Act of
Congress Bottle Glass

1971 Root Commemorative Bottle with Box &
Pres. Tag Glass

Blue Seltzer Bradford, Pa Glass   Green Seltzer Logansport IN Glass

1971 Display Bottle
w/cap Light Green
Glass 20"

1968 Display Bottle
w/cap Clear Glass
20"

1960's Display Bottle w/cap
Plastic Brown Paint 24"

Syrup Barrel w/paper label Wood
5 Gal.

1930's Display Bottle White
Chalk 20" High
Pat'd D105529

Pull apart Cork Screw-Opener
German Brass
5½" Long

Note pad holder w/music
box & Pen holder attached
Plastic 5" x 7"

1935 Coca-Cola
Glass 3⅞" High

Salesman Sample-Style Cooler
Some are empty, some have
thermos-bottles etc. Red Plastic
4 x 5 x 4"

Modified Flare
Glass 1920's
3¾" High

1934 Salesman Sample
"Open Front" Cooler Metal
8½ x 11 x 9"

"45" Record "Things go Better
with Coke" Plastic

45 Record Holder
Red Plastic

Red Metal Coke Carrier 1940's
(Rare)

Deep Yellow Carrier Coke
decal each end 1940's
(Rare)

Thermometer Porcelain
5¾ x 18"

Thermometer Tin Silhouette Girl
6½ x 16"

1960's Thermometer 18" Dia.

Tin Thermometer
Oval with Xmas Bottle
1938 6¾ x 16"

Thermometer Enjoy 1970's 18" Dia.

Thermometer 1950's
Metal 9"

Thermometer Gold
Bottle 1956 Metal 7½"

Thermometer 1950's 12" Dia.

Thermometer Tin Flat
Early 1950's 17"

Thermometer Wood
Circa 1905 5" x 21"

Thermometer Tin Xmas
Date 17" 1930's

2 Bottle Thermometer Tin
1942   7" x 16"

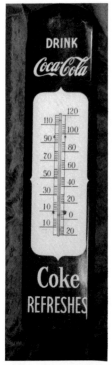

Cigar Shape
Thermometer Metal
30"

Wood Thermometer
5 x 21"

1940's Thermometer
Rare Porcelain 8 x 36"

Late 1940's Thermometer
Porcelain 2¼ x 9"

1945 Thermometer
Masonite 6¾ x 17"

All playing cards are listed in price guide

1-6

7-12

13-18

19-24

25-30

31-36

Silverware by
Straus Co.
Richmond VA
& Avon Plate

Paperweight Lucite 4⅜ x 4"

Paperweight-Bottle Cap Insert
1960's Glass 3" Dia.

Paperweight Spirit of 76 Glass
4" x 3"

Paperweight 1950 (very few
Originals) Glass 3½" x 2½"

Book Mark Owl Circa 1906
3⅛" x 1½"

Lillian Nordica Coupon with full page. (Full
page with coupon in original magazine more
valuable.) Paper 6½" x 9½"

Bridge Score Pad Circa 1944 Paper
Bound Volume of Pause Books

Matches are listed left to right-top to bottom

1950's Match Book	1960's Match Book
Match Book	1950's Match Book
1930's Match Book	1950's Match Book
1950's Match Book	Mid-1930's Match Book
1950's Match Book	1960's Match Book
1950's Match Book	1930's Match Book
1970's Match Book	Pair Dice

1970's White Santa
Stuffed Toy

1970's Black Skin Santa
Stuffed Toy

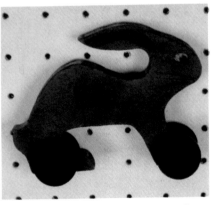

Rabbit Pull Toy - Rare Wood 3¾ x 4¾"

1940's Lighted Santa Claus Plastic
17" High

67

Arrow Sign Bottle 1930 Metal & Masonite 17" dia.

1950's Sign Lucite 21" x 15½"

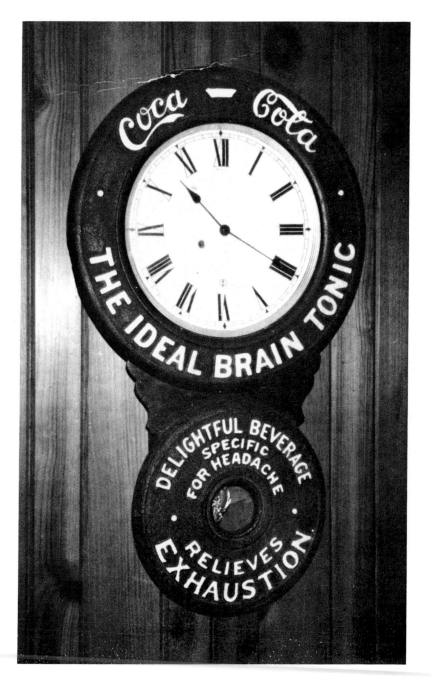

Baird Clock Wood Circa 1890

Betty Clock Pendulum Gilbert Circa 1910

Electric Clock Recent Plastic

Rocker Sign for Sidewalk Display 2 Sided Tin Sign in Metal Frame 20½ x 33½"

Miniature Bill Board Display
Cardboard Sign in Plastic Frame

Sign Fits on Top of Coke Bottle Display
Plastic 1950's

Santa Stand up Display (Many Versions)
Cardboard 6' Tall

Tin Sign Wood Frame 1935 30" x 72"

Straight Side Bottles Each end 1907 Rare Tin

Gas Today 1929 Tin 27" x 19"

1920's Cardboard Sign
Approx. 2' x 3'

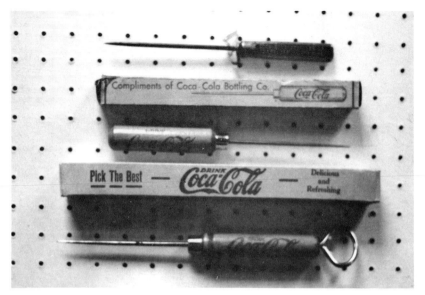

Ice Pick
Ice Pick in Box 1950's Metal Wood Handle
Ice Pick-Opener in Box 1930

Bottle Shaped Book Ends Circa 1950 Bronze

Self Framed Tin Sign 1917 20 x 30"

Hanging Sign 1904 8" Dia. Heavy Cardboard under Glass

33⅓ Record Jonathon Winter and Gene Rayburn 1960's

45 Record Eddie Fisher   45 Record Tony Bennett

45 Record Andrew Sisters Rum
& Coca-Cola

Sprite Boy Battery Operated Clock Plastic 1974

Sandwich Toaster Circa 1920'
Metal 7⅝ Dia.

Carrier for 4 Bottles 1960's Cardboard

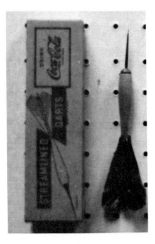

Box of Darts 1950's

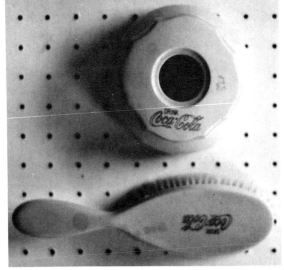

Hair Receiver 1930's Celluloid

Hair Brush 1930's Celluloid

12 Pencil Sharpeners (Full) Metal in Box

Pencil Sharpener Cast Iron Circa 1935's

6 Pack Holder 1950's Metal

6 Bottle Carrier Circa 1935 Cardboard

Holder for 6 Bottles 1950's Metal

6 Bottle Carrier 1940's Wood

6 Pack Carrier 1930's Cardboard

6 Bottle Carrier 1940's Divided Sections Wood

Opener Wall Mount 1920's
Opener Wall Mount
Opener Wall Mount Corkscrew
Opener Wall Mount Corkscrew and Hook
Opener Wall Mount 1950's

Child's Beach Seat 1950's Aluminum
Frame-cloth cover

Premix Bottle & Sleeve 1920's Glass

Lighted Sign 1960's Plastic Fram / Glass Face 8" Dia.

Hatchet & Knife 2 pieces Metal in Leather Case 1970's 10" long

Floating Fish Knife & Opener Metal & Wood 1960's 11"

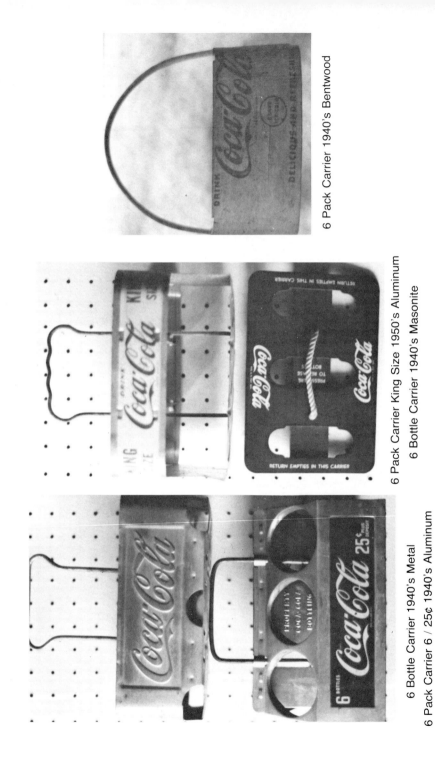

6 Pack Carrier 1940's Bentwood

6 Pack Carrier King Size 1950's Aluminum

6 Bottle Carrier 1940's Masonite

6 Bottle Carrier 1940's Metal

6 Pack Carrier 6 / 25¢ 1940's Aluminum

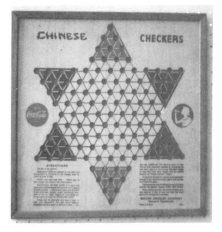

Chinese Checker Game Silhouette
Girl with Marbles Checker Board
Reverse Side Wood

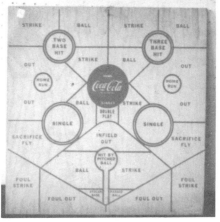

Baseball & Dart Board
Circa 1950 Sprite Box
Reverse Wood & Cork

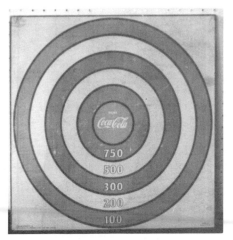

Dart Board 1935 Wood

Dispensing Machine in Box Plastic 1950's

Tic-Tac-Toe Game in Box
Winko Baseball Game w/ box and Board

Frizbee in Box Plastic

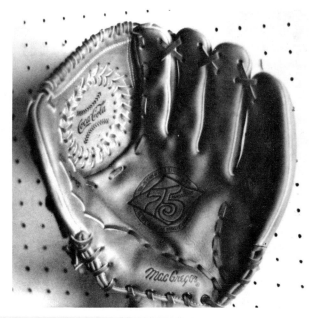

"Ball of Fame" American League on one side, National League
on other side Cardboard 9"

Baseball Glove Cincinnati OH 65th Anniv. Signed by Pete
Rose & Joe Morgan Leather

Miniature Dispenser & Bank 1950's Plastic

YoYo Duncan 1970's
YoYo Memphis Tenn.

Top Albany GA 1950's

Sprite Boy Domino's 1920's
Plastic

Coca-Cola Dispenser in Box 1960's Plastic

Domino's Coca-Cola Bottle Embossed on
each piece 1950's

Bingo Card Cardboard 1930's

Webster's Dictionary
"Little Gem" 1925
Leather Binding

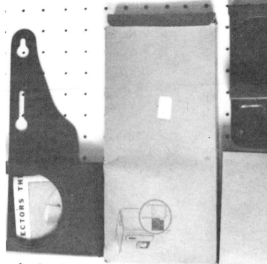

Dry Server Holder Attaches to Vending Machine Metal

Dry Server Holder Attaches to Vending Machine Metal

Inflatable Hanging Lite Plastic

Thermometer-Barometer Plastic

Price Guide

*All items are listed as they appear on the page,
left to right, top to bottom.*

SERVING & CHANGE TRAYS

Page 5
1901 - Change Tray $2000
1906 - $975
1909 - $650
1910 - $550

Page 6
1905 - Art Plate $450
1903 - $2400

Page 7-16
1913 - $450
1913 - Oval $750
1914 - $375
1914 - Oval $450
1917 - $200
1920 - Oval $650
1920 - $475
1921 - $475
1922 - $450
1923 - $200
1924 - $450
1925 - $175
1926 - $400
1927 - $300
1927 - Horizontal $250
1928 - $250
1929 - Glass $175

1929 - Bottle $300
1930 - Telephone $150
1930 - $160
1931 - Rockwell $450
1932 - $300
1933 - Francis Dee $225
1934 - $475
1935 - $125
1936 - $150
1937 - $85
1938 - $75
1939 - $65
1940 - $85
1941 - $90
1942 - $85
1948 - $50
1950's - $25

Page 17-18 Tip Trays
1909 - $260
1905 - $500
1907 - $375
1910 - $275
1913 - $150
1914 - $125
1917 - $125
1920 - $250

Trays Not Pictured In Book
1897 - 9¼" Dia. $5000
1898 - 9¼" Dia. Hilda Clark $5000
1899 - 9¼" Dia. Hilda Clark $3200
1899 - 6" Dia. $1800
1900 - 9¾" Dia. Bottle Tray $3600
1901 - 9¼" Dia. $2400
1901 - 5¼" Dia. Bottle $2600
1903 - 9¼" Dia. Hilda Clark $1650
1903 - 6" Dia. Hilda Clark $900
1903 - 4" Dia. Hilda Clark $800
1904 - 10½ x 13¼" Lillian Russell (Glass) $1100
1904 - 10½ x 13¼" Lillian Russell (Bottle) $1100
1905 - 10½ x 13¼" Juanita $1100
1908 - Topless $1600

Page 19
$1000
$800

Page 20
$275
$400
$600
$85

Page 21
$225
$235
$200
$700

Page 22
$55
$75
$65
$85

Page 23
$350
$275
$135

Page 24
$110
$85
$35

Page 25
$175
$75
$90
$70
$85

Page 26
$350
$75
$275
$60
$185

Page 27
$85
$45
$100

Page 28
$140
$80
$400

Page 29
$285
$60
$800
$800
650

Page 30
$170
$200
$185

Page 31
$70
$50
$425

Page 32
$135
$90
$75
$40
$85

Page 33
$275
$150
$750 (Rare)

Page 34
$250
$90
$75
$450

Page 35
1 - $ 85
2 - $ 60
3 - $ 85
4 - $ 65
5 - $ 75
6 - $ 75
7 - $ 90

8 - $ 50
9 - $ 40
10 - $110
Plastic Frame & Bottle $90
11 - $ 85
12 - $ 85
13 - $ 25
14 - $ 85
15 - $ 75
16 - $ 75

Page 36 & 37
COCA-COLA CALENDARS

1891 - $4700
1892 - $4700
1897 - $2800.
1900 - $5000
1901 - $2000
1902 - $1400
1903 - $1000
1907 - $1000
1910 - $1300
1911 - $1100
1913 - $875
1914 - $425
1915 - $570
1916 - $350
1917 - $485
1918 - $650
1919 - $425
1920 - $350
1921 - $300
1922 - $300
1923 - $200
1924 - $250
1925 - $200
1926 - $325
1927 - $250
1928 - $240
1929 - $335
1930 - $375
1931 - $325
1932 - $165
1933 - $155
1934 - $160
1935 - $185
1936 - $185
1937 - $175

1938 - $150
1939 - $150
1940 - $150
1941 - $55
1942 - $60
1943 - $60
1944 - $60
1945 - $65
1946 - $50
1947 - $50
1947 - Boy Scout $250
1948 - $55
1949 - $50
1950 - $50
1951 - $35
1952 - $50
1953 - $50
1954 - $50
1955 - $40
1956 - $40
1957 - $55
1958 - $35
1959 - $35
1960 - $20
1961 - $20
1962 - $25
1963 - $25
1964 - $25
1965 - $25
1966 - $25
1967 - $25
1968 - $25
1969 - $25
1970 - $15
1971 - $15
1972 - $15
1973 - $15
1974 - $15
1975 - $15
1976 - $15
1977 - $10
1978 - $15
1979 - $10
1980 - $10
1981 - $10
1982 - $10
1983 - $10
1984 - $10

1985 - $10

Page 38
$30
$35
$20

Page 39
$475
$90
$125
$25
$20
$95
$35

Page 40
1 - $125
2 - $80
3 - $30
4 - $60
5 - $75
6 - $25
7 - $60
8 - $145
9 - $70
10 - $85
11 - $85
12 - $15
13 - $145

Page 41
$75
$225
$225
$60
$45
$20
$435
$400

Page 42
$140
$775
$850
$20

Page 43
$135
$100

Page 44
$75
$90
$85
$85
$165

Page 45
$75
$65
$35
$85
$60
$75

Page 46
$75
$30
$175
$75
$125
$150
$280 (Composition $500)
$30
$100

Page 47
$4300
$1600
$400
$350

Page 48
$1200
$950
$125
$600

Page 49 Pocket Mirrors

1905 - $285
1906 - $285
1908 - $525
1909 - $275
1910 - $235
1911 - $220
1913 - $290
1916 - $210
1920 - $300
1922 - $1000

Page 50
$75
$150
$150 each piece

Page 51
$90
$30
$35
$400
$35
$85

Page 52
1 -$100
2 - $40
3 - $25
4 - $25
5 - $30
6 - $30
7 - $135
8 - $35

Page 53 OPENERS ETC.
1 - $25
2 - $35
3 - $10
4 - $15
5 - $35
6 - $80
7 - $15
8 - $45
9 - $75
10 - $8
11 - $15
12 - $15
13 - $20
14 - $10
15 - $100
16 - $75
17 - $35
18 - $60
19 - $25
20 - $75
21 - $100

Page 54
1 - $12
2 - $10

3 - $18
4 - $22
5 - $10
6 - $15
7 - $6
8 - $20
9 - $14
10 - $9
11 - $15
12 - $14
13 - $12
14 - $10

Page 55
Trade Card $450
Blotters
$85
$75
Dated $50
Dated $50
Dated $50
Dated $50
Not Dated $30
Not Dated $30
Not Dated $30
Not Dated $30
$40
$15
$10
$15
$45
$10
$5
$5
$5
$5
$5
$5
$5
$3

Page 56
$75
$275
$130
$225

Page 57
$95

$80
$65
$130
$300

Page 58
$200
$115
$30
$65
$60

Page 58
$200
$115
$30
$65
$60

Page 59
$750
$30
$6
$65
$65

Page 60
$120
$85
$135
$75

Page 61
$110
$45
$17
$75

Page 62
$30
$425
$110
$95

Page 63
$300
$60
$375
$75
$100

Page 64

All Prices Based on Full Deck & Jokers.
Decks unopened will increase value.

1 - 1909 $450
2 - 1928 $300
3 - 1938   Softbox (Red) $75
4 - 1938   Hardbox (Red) $75
5 - 1938   Hardbox (Blue) $75
6 - 1943 $55
7 - 1943 $50
8 - 1943 $55
9 - 1943 Airplane Spotter $55
10 - 1943 Regular $75
11 - 1943 Yellow Border $60
12 - 1943 Blue Border $65
13 - Blue $75
14 - 1951 $55
15 - 1951 $50
16 - 1956 $45
17 - 1956 $45
18 - 1958 $45
19 - 1958 $45
20 - 1959 $45
21 - 1959 $45
22 - 1960 $55
23 - 1960 $45
24 - 1961 $55
25 - 1961 $45
26 - 1963 $45
27 - 1963 $65
28 - 1963 $35
29 - 1963 $35
30 - 1971 Boy Scout $75
31 - 1971 $15
32 - 1971 $15
33 - 1971 Mexico $20
34 - 1974 $8
35 - 1974 $8
36 - 1976 $10

Page 65
$60-$80 per Piece
$35
$20
$75
$25
$500

$100
$15
$18

Page 66

$3, $3, $7, $3, $4,

$2, $1, $2, $3, $2,

$6, $3, $12,

$5

Page 67
$50
$35
$250
$250

Page 68
$175
$65

Page 69
$3500

Page 70
$25
$1500

Page 71
$125
$15
$40
$25-$75

Page 72
$135
$700
$200

Page 73
$700

Page 74
$5
$8
$15
$90 Pr.

Page 75
$1000
$350

Page 76
$18
$8
$12
$20

Page 77
$40
$600

Page 78
$15
$55
$65
$55
$425
$30 ea.

Page 79
$20
$15
$40
$35
$20
$40

Page 80
$40
$100
$8
$25
$40
$10
$65
$40

Page 81
$110
$75
$20

Page 82
$40
$25
$20
$30
$40 Bentwood

Page 83
$60
$55
$75

Page 84
$50
$85
$85
$25 Frizbee

Page 85
$45
$100

Page 86
$90
$10
$8
$6
$10

Page 87
$25
$40
$20
$25

Page 88
$60
$60
$30
$20

AN INVITATION TO JOIN

THE COLA CLAN is an international organization of people dedicated to the study of the history and the collecting of the memorabilia of The Coca-Cola Company.

THE COLA CLAN provides:
- Nationwide and international communication among Coca-Cola collectors
- Increased markets for buying, trading, and selling collectables
- Comprehensive bi-monthly newsletter
- Alternate bi-monthly want ad supplement
- Free advertising in newsletter and want ad supplement
- Local chapters
- Annual convention

ANNUAL DUES for primary membership in The Cola Clan are $15.00. Additional members of your family or company who would like to become eligible to vote, run for office, and receive merchandise offered on a 'per membership' basis, may buy an associate membership for $5.00 per year. The associate member will be entitled to the same rights and privileges of primary membership except for receiving The Cola Clan publications which are mailed to primary members only.

If you wish to join, complete and return this form with one year's dues to:

Alice Fisher
The Cola Clan Treasurer
2084 Continental Drive N.E.
Atlanta, Georgia 30345

_____ $15
Primary Member's Name (type or print one name only)

_____
Street Address, Box #, Route #

_____
City, State, Zip Code

_____
Area Code — Telephone Number

_____ $5
Associate Member's Name — Relationship

_____ $5
/81 Associate Member's Name — Relationship

95